~~~

Flux Kingdom

~~~

Patrick Denton Mackay

JAKE BOOKS 2011

ISBN-10: 09-678151-7-7
ISBN-13: 978-0-9678151-7-6

Flux Kingdom

JAKE BOOKS

Below the Frequency of Light (CD)
Deadpan
Experimental Music
The Book of Jake
The No Theater
Flux Kingdom

CONTENTS

Flux Kingdom

Jack Matter

Wards

Bulletproof

Reich Deposition

Flux Documentation

Flux Kingdom

Channel Crossing (Normandy, June 6, 1944)

When I was in the center of the pool I was afraid that I'd lose my voice, but I lost my voice to fire and the pool was my heart and the pool was every voice. I was the impossible of the channel of a million voices and they came through in water, song-full and on fire with the light of my fear. When I lost my voice, when I un-became every body of rage, every promise, clear as the origin of man—this cared and carried my hate deep. I was afraid to hate. My love was afraid. I feared for the life of my hate. It hurt like ice. Frozen in disbelief, I sharpened my guts to metal. My voice became my Fai'y and I melted in the song of my hatred. I did not know that my hatred was my love. I did not know that my ice was my fire. But I knew, however, that my song, lost in the pool of voices, was a sword. Every emotion. Every emotion in my gut was the ice of Fai'y. Every voice killed me a little and I could not melt my fear. Why does fire and ice compliment the most hideous and beautiful making? In the pool my voice answered. I heard love hating. I felt my sing as a blade in the guts of my fear. When I knew this I was released from the pool and the coalesce of water that shed from my eyes was infinite. In this moment I realized that my fear, ice sharp and ready, could use her love to kill, and the hate, deep as my longing for voice, was relentless, deep, and absolute. My poem cut the throat of my enemies with the most promising hate, of which my love sung. And this was my poem relieved of the voices. And this was my love relieved from not knowing how to hate. And I could not ever fear again because my love and her sharp sword of hate were absolute. I am, for this reason, still alive.

The Kingdom

Resonances. The table blooms. The walls white. It is raining purity in columns of architecture. I meet you here and we practice writing. The river un-runs it. Speech is the empty force of in-between that stitches our feelings. Feelings un-rupture into rings and real blue. I stand without you not knowing. So, here, the engraved nowhere greens out in striations and we touch the language with our eyes. How long has it been since you have felt your home? In no time I answer. Everywhere bears down into the node of the architecture. Full of fluid, the columns are climbed by light. I feel ill. The light falls about me in kingdom. We survive in the mistake. See the black burgeon and concentrate into a spot. We are ink. Coalesce of love books into the column. They wrap around, pages of texture in the stand. You turn and see the light green bend into comma. Your lips respond that way and the air puffs out like plumes.

Practical Matters of Royalty

Someone, somewhere, is a king. If I were a king I would knight my men. After all were knighted I would take a walk. The stars are ubiquitous. My men are unseen. In the daytime my knights disappear. So, as king, angels appear in the light. When I close my eyes I am knighted and the angels are kings. When I walk at dusk or early morning, my angels prepare for the knights. Or themselves. At this time I am a metaphor. Everything, like the crack on the horizon, goes through me—Angels, Knights, Elves, and Fai'y. My lips are gold. I speak the truth. The truth is the center of the king. Hence, if there is no God, I rule for my men, for my women, for imagination, to pass through. The truth is that the language is king. Speech, in a turn, crowns the innocent with life.

Interpretation of Narnia

The spell that I am under is Narnia. The rest of the world is a bulldozer. When I awake there will be the reverse of Narnia. "Ainran". My priest is aware that the world is on the brink. All my power, Aslan, is in your paw. This is a lie. Edmond is Androcles. The thorn was withdrawn by Edmond. Edmond lost himself to the White Witch. But when Edmond recovered he went to Aslan and pulled the thorn from his paw. The thorn preempted the cru-cif-ix-ion of Aslan. So, when the White Witch tries to pin Aslan down, by the hand of Edmond, the misspelling of Aslan as "Ainran", repays the nail through a metaphor in Edmond to the White Witch. In this manner Edmond saved the crown. Edmond is a prince. The Turkish Delight failed.

Aroshel and Lattarice

I want to know my exact identity instead of being everybody else. You are light. You are clearly deep. You are in the abyss. Someone wants a sword. If you draw me and hold me like love I will love you forever. I have not been held in eleven years. I am tired of fighting, yet I want to end their existence. My attributes are multiple. The attribute I am working on is my sword. I have put it into Orion's sheath. We now know each other as friends, Taurus and Orion. Yet I would never put my sword there. I could never put it in my mouth or song either. The only place I would have put Aroshel is in a place where no other could find her. Hide in plane sight. This is safest. I would only have put her into a metaphor, the slip in time where everything changes. I am really good with metaphors. This means she is here but hidden. I know that only the right hand can hold her. I say her like a ship. Metal and fire make swords. I am mettle and I have no fire. Then it must be ice. The metaphor of ice is crystal, eyes, and water. I hate crystal, love eyes, and live in water. Then Aroshel only needs me to see like crystal. I am too tired to see so many wars. Then the crystal must be one thing. If I am surrounded by water in fantasy that is real and everywhere there are eyes and my queen is the ocean, then my sword is in the ocean. This is where, on the cliffs of Cornwall, Arthur, my grandfather, would have cast Aroshel. His name for the sword was Sally. When he threw Sally into the sea he was communicating to me to go forth into the sea. If Arthur knew that the largest body on the planet would take his love he would want his muse to spread into her. This means that he wants for my sword to kill. Aroshel has not killed before. Sally is the name for Charley. Charley is the name for Lattarice. Lattarice is the Fai'y name for Gabriel. Gabriel holds the light of the blade. The blade is only known by one name. No one knows this name unless it slays them. My grandfather is forgiven for letting them know its name. Aroshel is the prince's name for L'eshora. My sword is shore. I mean sure. I need not go anywhere to find this other than my sea, which lies before me in blue pools.

Sword Documentation

If I have tried once and failed I must try again. I have said it is my song. I have said my blade is my lips. I have said I am king. Yet my sword is not here. Time has been broken. In the gap of time there is a lake. The lake holds all in reflection. One would think that this is where the sword is. Here or in the stone. I have the mark of the cup. I see this as a chalice and also a sword. From my head down to my loins, guard to point. Then, the only way to use my sword is to fuck. This is true. Yet, in the lake is one reflection. This reflection is real and fantasy, which means it—the fantasy—is real and the real is a vicissitude. At the right moment in time, in the right name, with the right history, like a combination lock, the lake will spill. I know this because I have drawn her before. So before me I now know the future. The specific individual will, at the right moment, draw Aroshel from the abyss. Simplicimus is the code word for the address to the Pope. At the point of reflection the song will withdrawal the lake into a sword. At this point time will become together and there will be a great battle that is realized truly.

"To Bring Them To Bear"

Sinking deep into your truth, the truth that you can hold, your center of emotion, demand the universal scale. Once you achieve your vision of the scale, if during the day, bring yourself to the ocean and read your soul. From your soul demand the ocean to procure Aroshel. Your voice will raise her if true. When Aroshel has achieved you you will either be slain or forgiven. Only the exact song will save your life. When your song is exact (in doubt, fear, love…) Aroshel will bury herself in your truth. This is the gift. Open and give yourself the present Fai'y. (You must rest for one day.) The next night, wait for Orion to rise. Align yourself with the Atlas and withdraw from Orion's belt Selinquel. You will then know the truth. The next day, go to the ocean and say the right words for Lattarice. When you cry you have conceived her. Aroshel, in this manner, will be clear. Let yourself go. Don't know anything. Your action will welc Lattarice with Aroshel. Then from yourself, draw both edges. This can only be put together with the right recipe.

Milk Cure

This is written on the real full moon. The milk that was the story that cured the edge of Aroshel after she was taken from the abyss of fire tempered her edge. At night this is the white of the poem around Lattarice. At night Lattarice is named Selinquel. Selinquel tells her sharp story to the word. All night long Selinquel answers the demons of the third world. When, during the day, Aroshel has been worked in the foundry of the sun she is sure and therefore L'eshora. The milk of the moon in daylight is pure song, and purely turns in the feel of the light. The milk cures the edge of reality known to the real world as false. My friends do not want to change. I know Lattarice Selinquel cures both worlds and the third, where demons come from. To cure the demons you turn the song and the milk of the moon answers Fai'y. In Fai'y lore the song is the sword of trust. If you do not trust then the edge blinds you. You can see how I cannot see any of the work. My blindness is my trust. Therefore I am of sword. Aroshel, Lattarice, and Selinquel (day, storm, and night) all tune together their meaning. Each answers all of my music and spirit exactly.

A Dream Battle

I have failed. I can't write against it. They have taken
everything. Lip dust. Soul shake. I am the sum of the horrible
world. Torn pieces of paper in the gutter. Failed. Failed. Up
against the wall. Back to the stone. An erased sunset…from
my song I draw the stone. My back burned, cold, freezing. The
hordes bearing down. I press against the wall. I see nothing.
Still as the ice of winter. Bearing down on me. Bearing down
in their mass, the black bodiless souls of time. All I feel is the
rain. From the stone I draw my stone. It won't sing. It is singing.
My steel! I can't see. My breath is frozen. I am alone. I think of
my family and banish my family. Alone. My song falters. The
stone turns to dust in my hand. What horrible mixtures of life!
They bear down. I am alone. I am blind. The stone in my hand
steel. The steel in my hand light. The light in my hand ready.
Bitter! Bitter! Bitter! I slake my sword's hunger. Brilliant light!
Blinding. Press into the edge. I am aware of light only. Terrible.
Terrible as my spirit!

Mirror School

I hate myself purely. This is the test. Bitterness, a form of love, frees life. I have my eye upon the stone. Most people think Excalibur is the name of the sword. Only a fool would name her. Only a fool would put a sword in a stone. I turn and the forest leaves me. I turn again and the lake is shivering. When I turn for a third time the lake is a mirror. Lady, forgive me, you are without the right place. Lift up my reflection and you will see what the nameless is. Like that. You hold my body still. I think I am the sword; I am the archetype of the sword. If I were the sword I would have to slay demons with my edge. Please forgive me, lady. My edge is only my lips. They have stolen centuries. Hence, when you hold me, everybody coalesces into the mirror and I am burned with the mark of your gift. Take her from me! My poem continues. I am the sword and I have mistaken the mirror for a lake. You bring me up. I am taken by the air. The air is a song. I am tempered by the nature of this gift. What I want is the absolute right of my nature! The words say calm. No one holds me save the air. I am struck hard and forged in memory. When I recall the beauty of my past, yellow light. When I recall the history, bitter, freezing weather. The weather is my edge. I am pure almost. In reflection, I see the sword released. The shape is who I am. All I need to do is pull from my truth this beauty.

The Exchange of Lattarice for Farina
"Water Gift"

One of my eyes is Cockney. When I look it is a lake that cannot
see. When I close my eye, the Cockney music shows me the
kingdom. Phosphorescence. Endless light. The promise of
Aroshel turning in the poem of a stream. I have been afraid to
speak my mind. My Cockney has drowned in the no music.
When my mind speaks it speaks softly. My spell I am under is
the house of Atreides. I have met the Fremen and they know
the spell is true. In my understanding Aroshel is light, hence
not a Kris Knife. Yet the Fremen have welcomed me and they
have seen the edge. In exchange for Apollo's light they have
given me the black edge knife of the desert. In the night it is
blue. You know the blade by how it speaks. I give the Fremen
Lattarice's sorrow and they return me in kind the most loyal
gift. Her name is Farina. Farina is the name of the blue edge of
trust. It can cut through all metal. The water of Lattarice is my
tears. Aroshel I hold up to Apollo. Apollo takes the edge and
makes Alphine on the cure. I put the blade to the wounded
nameless…"I son will be born"…I utter. The wound in the gap
of time they know is cauterized. I am blind. The blue light edge
is at my neck…"Translate your soul"…I take this in and show
them my eyes. We are in agreement with the song and the knife
is withdrawn. In this manner Farina is absolute loyalty. In this
manner I know my friends.

The Instrument of Aroshel and Lattarice

I have been into several storms. The real storm is easy (let the tempest tell you secrets). The psychical storm, otherwise known as hell, is much more challenging. Every conceivable doubt about reality strips the will. At best you are completely bereft of idea. At best you are without action conceivable. Buddha was in the latter. Jesus Christ was in the former. When I see the rain in the street each drop is a broken blade. Who could shatter Aroshel but the gods who gifted her. All of my desire plummeting to the earth in shards. What I know of Aroshel is that if she breaks she becomes Lattarice. Lattarice is the name of the sad storm—"the tears of sadness". When Aroshel is broken, Lattarice reforms in the earth: puddles, lakes, ocean, streams—all in the dark of the storm filled. When the day comes, Lattarice, in the lambent scintillation of the sun, waves and comes together. At this moment Aroshel is returned. I lift her from the lake with my eyes. The blade is keen enough to kill. My song in my eyes raises her green and engrailed. When it is time I will look to the west and Aroshel Lattarice, one blade of rain and one of sun, will be drawn from Apollo. In this way Apollo gives the Fai'y dark Elvin instrument of justice to the poets.

Jack Matter

~~~

There must be a poem that is deeper than Valentine's Day. Saint Valentine and the horrible massacre we all know. These two points never cross. You cannot cross your hell with your heaven. If you cross heaven you get hell. If you cross hell you get heaven. You, my undying love, have crossed hell. What heaven has left for you is impossible. To know the word impossible is to know that the poem that is impossible is an act of love. What did you do for this love? What did you do that was the ultimate beauty of nature? You went to hell for love and left your love at home to save her. She is now in your words like a glint of knowledge that she would know you from the billion problems on earth; know you so absolutely all you have to do is turn away and she is there. How do you hold her? How do you trust? Live…her lips are your mouth, complete.

~~~

The clue to life is to live. The clue to death is don't die.
The clue to love is to know. The clue to feeling is to know
that death will never conquer life. When I feel this I am
skeptical as hell. They poisoned me when I was drinking.
I collapsed in an elevator and when I died I knew that the
clue to feeling is that life that is known both lives and dies.
How could I love my own decision to poison myself out of
love? Tristan, when he achieved his story, died for Isolde.
Romeo, when he achieved love, stupidly killed himself in
sorrow. I am alive today because my sorrow could not kill.
Hence poison, the cup of sorrow that all drink, is only the
idea of death, but not death really. So when I drank like
Dylan my final drinks, I was aware that my death needed
life. What death could want such a thing? I drowned my
sorrow in a cup. The cup was my trust. When I awoke, I,
Giants fan, lush, linguist, poet, looked out of your eyes.
This poem that I am writing is my home run.

~~~

Recovering is a drag. I am within me filling from my well. Blue. Freezing. One way to go. His eyes are scales that weigh the sun. Mine are songs and my songs have wings. Where may I fly to? How many woman know these songs? One drop of me in the middle of my heart. I have not been here before. I don't know the rules. My secrets are open. My open is raw. Be the sun in the pool flickering out her rings of well light. If I drink the abyss I am no worse off than if I drink my own blood. Loyalty? I will shun all alliances…even to myself. The trust shakes in the pool, like an unknown child. How can I tell him that he need not reflect the shit of the world? How may I disclose the shit of the world as love? The women pass by like wax candles, their sex frozen in my lake. What I trust is how deep I have hurt. This I trust because, like this pool, it is pure with my entire spell of pain. If this pain is the water of my life then I have accomplished my life: love, depth, innocence, reality, reflection, pain.

~~~

Tons of people erase the street. I move in a comma. My
knowledge of commas is the same as the people—People
erase and gather time; commas erase and gather pools.
Look, you are in one. Look again, you are time. See time
quiver in her elastic water, in her reflection. You can drink
time. A comma drinks me. People that love life eventually
use a comma. Commas space people out. The pool of time
is crying upward. The result is rain; our rain in reverse
because time lived is in reverse. At the center of time there
is no clock, just like at the center of people there is no
heart. Yet, put a word in the center of a person and they
see time. Time shivers like concentric rings outward into
the edge of a comma. I am collecting the sound. It does
not speak life. I cannot see death. The edge whispers with
people and time whispers with the pool. Flow this truth
down into the water in the earth. It is about time that
people knew what time is. I am afraid to finish this poem.

~~~

Before the Nazis come, give me a kiss. There, they are at
our door. They love to burn children and adults, disabled
people, and dogs who inform. Invite them in. Please, have
a seat. Look at all of our art. I think we know you from
WWII, WWI, and the Romans. Please, sit next to the fire
and get warm. We will tell you secrets. Look, do you see
this pot; it was fired at 1000 degrees and then spun on a
wheel where my mother glazed the skin. Much like your
work! How joyful it is to have you here! Please, have a
drink! It is Absinthe 1939! After the Putsch! We wanted of
it to be a better gravity so we put it in a tumbler and spun
it at 1000 MHz and it came out as bitter as my family line.
Pour yourself reality. I will pour it for you. What is the
best thing? All of us are in a circle. We are at the center.
You are around us. You and I can see my tattoos. They
are "Freedom", "War", and "Truth". I toast all of you. My
dear friends. Please, let me take a picture, I will light a fire.
There, all together in front of the fire! Click!

~~~

The juke box opens with the Sex Pistols. I hate the Sex
Pistols. I hate the juke box. I even hate these tourists
because they ask nothing to be everything. I am pulling
the trigger to the next volume. I am channeling the click.
Do you know how long I have been waiting for you from
the general morass? Now. Now is the turn of the chamber.
Deal me a card. Deuces are slop. Spades are for after
night. I see in fours. Call me anytime. I am as here as a
fucking whore prints your war with want. I am as well
aimed as my punctuation. Leave out the coalesce visitors
and become a nervous wreck. We have dived deep. Look.
I have dived deep look to soul deep this answer. One
hundred Nazis within one body. One hundred demons in
the brain. Who will be the first to laugh? Me? You? Or is
my hate deeper. My sword, Orion, is replaced by the day.
Your bow, Orion, is replaced by Diana. Diana cannot be
replaced. My immaculate brethren. Please look into the air.
Oh, The juke box opens with the Sex Pistols, another name
for shaft, which is the exact name for the silver tip that was
played by Hermes so Apollo could receive his lyre.

~~~

When we have nothing we either fuck or we fight. At the bar, the words of my friends an echo. When we go out we either fuck or we fight. If when we fuck we fight, our women get laid. If when we fight we fuck, their women get laid. If we do nothing then everybody is fucked. Hence we are fucking fighters and fighting fuckers and nothing, the universal reference, is perfectly poised to be fucked for fighting for us. Why, you ask? Because it is the best ref. Should we fuck fighters or fight fuckers or simply fuck the ref? If the ref is a fucker then we'll have him fight for us. If the ref is a fighter then we'll have him fucked seven times a day seven days a week until he sees god. If the ref is god and he fucks us then we'll fuck him back. If god is a fighter then we'll fight him back. And, if the world doesn't yet know how to fuck and fight then we'll teach them that there is no god.

~~~

I am listening, but I don't have the time. Is listening a matter of time? Yes, but not the way you think. Unconceive your methods. Be alien. Be forgetful. Be lost. On the other side of every coin is another coin. Trick. Look at this quarter. See the eagle, the president, and the silver? What is in the flip when the homeless men flip the thing? I see one bird, one pool, one reflection of monetary eternity. Keep flipping your perception until you choose your teacher. I would not be here without the turn, the turn you made in the immaculate books of your life. Flip this even and watch the pages choose a word. What word? Now. In this way when you flip you are exactly stitched together by your feeling. Now 1944. Now 1851. Now 2011. Put your flip sense into the picture and punk your lips to blow the wind out like royalty. Give me the bank and I will give you the emptiness. You see one friend in reflection and a billion ways to not interpret life. Why? Because at this bank love is life and life is won.

~~~

Dank as a vow, undreamed in the age, solemn and old and fit with a million boxes, letter strung, lung wet with wit, postal my beauty, office of on, sun sinned and full with the solution of word…I am in the letter pusher's pen of beauty. Air redolent with history. Slow as a tomb. Curved as the letters standing in line. Save this sanctuary God from the Christians in their blitzkrieg tech center church. Lock out the rich. Bar the scene. Sip the air and live in the line of the heathen peddlers of fate, the druggies, the mugs, the homeless, the rakes, poets and artists of forever. Keep this place dirty with the letter of life. More comfortable than a cool pool reflect the sentience of letter ten million times. The wick of this candle bitter trove sucks the truth in and holds the ceremony of life. The dream we never possessed in veritas. Put your mail in the safe and save its lines with the angle of light, your key to the dark.

~~~

The problem is that there is no problem. We have fallen. They have fallen. What has fallen is never easy. I want to laugh because of the pit, the pit where I have fallen to is a metaphor. How can you have a fruit with such sweet veins, the orange the tree, the tree the sound, the sound the light! Here I think. Hear me think life is death and death is life and the concept in-between, the bridge, is the light of my soul uncorrupted. All I want, however, is to sink into the pit and know that there are no sides, that there is just seed.

Wards

~~~

Nothing was my friend. We'd disappear together as opposites. When I remembered all the shit in the world, it would be there waiting at the corner to undo my all. When I was a painting it would put me on the wall and my back would press through like a faint glow at dusk. Then, turning my light off, in a kiss, I would un-become the museum. There are no words for this. It felt like sinking, sinking into an ocean until the sun disappeared. I would laugh, then fall through the mirror like Alice. Yet I would not be Alice. I was the Mad Hatter. My clock would tell every time. I had a million words for one thing and none for everything. In this museum I grew. I learned that Lewis Carroll was trying to save Alice Liddell on the Thames where my grandfather and I floated, seaming up the stitch that times London. You can save everyone with the right words. You can save yourself by unmaking insane. You can be no ocean off in the museum by unthinking your factory system of not reality. Nothing matters more than everything. My friend, you are looking at a painting of water. The painting is fake; the water is real.

~~~

I am looking every which way. Multitudinal and absolute.
I am looking every which way because I am a trigger to
reality. People think I am a dream. I am also a real dream.
When the shit goes down my focus is every which way
yet my poem, the trigger, is perfect. My eye, a finger of
perfection, is waiting. Sure as my doubt and pure as my
reflection I, with myself on the poem, wait. My poems are
slow. My eye is fast. My soul is pure. What I know is that
the devil exists, angels are real, the church is bad, love is
purer as hatred, and my poem is the answer to all of this.
When the priest in the guise of a devil enters, my hand,
my eye, and my pen are sure. When the devil in the guise
of a priest enters I am even surer. At this moment every
direction converges on the crosshairs of my conscience.
Pure as my muse, my muse the bullet in the gun, the
words in my poem the bullets of my promise, I pull the
circle around me, make a cross, and the chamber empties.
When I say, you are a poet you know the absolute you live.
I blow smoke from the barrel and the question: Who could
convene in such hideous forms! Intuitively, the asking
fluxes and the multitude of words silver as truth turn
cylindrical in the ears of my guilt. You see meaning open
up and salt the story in a blanket of ocean.

~~~

This inverse reality knows one thing: if you point the dream gun at the real it is real; if you point the real gun at the dream it is not. Hence, I am a dream. The mechanisms in my hand are confusing. At one moment birds, at another moment a cross, at another a nine-millimeter Browning. The children come and take in their hands the birds. The church comes and takes the cross. My muse keeps writing for the gun. When the children take the bird it is a sign of innocence. When the church takes the cross it is a sign of terror. When my muse takes the gun it is a sign of poetry. My hand never wanted any of this. I look across at my gifts. The church is very happy to have a cross. The children are very curious about the birds. My muse can only aim for the cross because the cross is a focus. I ask them to haul it up and give me a target. Two nuns and two priests arrange the wood up on the altar. Accidentally, the birds of the children explode in the air. My muse, never one to hold a gun, pulls the trigger, startled by the present. Bang! Bang! Bang! Bang! When the birds clear, two nuns and two priests lie dead at the altar. Never accept a gift that you cannot live up to.

~~~

I have been marked for life. My sign is anti-infinity. I will
live for my making. My moment will be a word. If the
dictionary possesses my body and each word is a minute.
I will have 33, 210 minutes of life. Fuck time. Make it all
converse into one second, 33,210 words plunging deep into
my spirit. Light compounds of voice! Splintering meaning
of life! Plunge into me and focus my meaning! Meaning be
my life downloaded into my spirit! Call the Angels. Call
the Devils. Call the Sprites, the Fai'y, the Elves. Look at me,
my wellbeing the flux light. See the rivulets of definition
blitz out to the edges. I am building myself alone. I am,
as the other millions of words crash my hard drive, one
thing. What is the meaning of a child wanting to hold the
universe in their mouth? The truth is unkind. The falseness
is special. The fact, my muse, is this: I love you, love you
more than the universe, more than the ocean; more even
than myself. I open, true as the scintillating floral electric in
my soul, deep. From depths universal my words in love.

~~~

What I have found are unabsolute truths. What is absolute
is the "un". I "un" then everything. I am not ashamed to
not be. The beauty of nature is not abashed to be without.
The church is not guilty to lack. Even God has his faults.
Ungodly acts are more defined than Godly ones. Be good,
my son, for the truth is that if God exists he is disabled.
I pray to people in wheelchairs, lunatics, lepers, sick
children, and my own schizoaffective attribute. Please tell
the mistaken universe that God is moored in the harbor
behind the eyes of the plague victims of 1666. Please tell
the church that behind the tongues of invalids is the word.
Please tell the destitute that they only need graffiti their
neighborhood with this truth. We will see each other in jail
and the priest will come to anoint us. Yet, when the door
closes he will have to ask himself how he, too, is disabled,
to distinguish between the multiple criminal lost priests
who now begin to prey on him. And one Parkinson patient
who shakes uncontrollably will respond to his prayer:
Yes Father, you may now illuminate me about Africa, The
Middle East, Spain, South America, Germany, the Native
Americans…and tell me your dream of the conversion of
pain into gold, and your disease into capital, make me still.

~~~

I am slow. I out not snails. I don't yes cars. I flunk
emotional school. The path of my making is a static radio.
You may hear the waves take away the shoreline. We are
delivered to our gods in Tai Chi. The moment I succumb
to the stone of my being I am a limpet. I hold on for life.
Confusion is fast. Like a flicker in the resilient beauty
of a candle in church. Confused by the light blanketing
Jesus. Where you see this the lambent majesty of his
form is unstrung in the light. Fast flickers of tongue that
makes him angelic. He…he must burn inside with the
same slow passion of the nails holding him up. He must
be the message of how and who we are, strung in the
wires of the future. I don't want to write this. I wanted to
say the candles are friends. Don't show me a God I must
think through to know. The light chips away at his dead
conscience like a snake's tongue keeping him well, like
prayers.

~~~

This is a ward poem. I pull it to the root to back see the
slime. Phlegm means fire. I sickness in the light reflect.
Reflect light in the sickness of I. Word. Turn slowly
all around the root. You see nothing in conception.
Conception sees nothing in you. This, interwoven with the
poison of a stare. Eat me. Ecila. How I ask you will. Turn
the 1851 sentience around like a word. Eighteen Fifty-One.
One fifty aid in…Now over into your wetware eat ware
no here love. Evolve flow in the reflect of Alice. Again,
die your own soul black with my words reverse and clean
as the apple in your throat, like Old English devolving
in your pate. Blind open and clear as this line. Annihilate
yourself in your knowledge of myself.

~~~

Lisp. Song of the snake. Venomous gays. Beautiful snakes. I have a Ferret named "Deep Song". I stick Deep Song in the hole. He is beautiful. I let Deep Song go, up the hole in the sky. The beauty of Deep Song. I am marked by three poems: "Snake", "Game," and, "Deep Song". Snake is deep in the hole. Deep Song has Game and plunges up the ass in the sky. I can hear him singing, like Ferrets do, the grunt of the hunt. He is hungry for the whole snake! He is ravenous for the poem! Deep Song, up the ass in the sky like a king! But I cannot see anything. He is gone like the wind. Then a ton of grunting like a Pimp in bed with a trick. "Game" and him fucking the snake over in the dark. I plunge my hope into the ass of the poem and Deep Song eats the ass of the snake, like a story. Two minutes. Then, from the hole, a beautiful poem!

~~~

My final poem would be one weed in a field of concrete with a sign on it that said, "Happy New Year!" Who knows how the weed got there; and with a device attached that could obliterate a lot. I study this weed, slow and deep like my love. I study him like I would a black witch in the church. It is beautiful and lithe and holy as the lot. In full attention it looks like a piece of seaweed, brown and open to the sun. I am very excited because of this poem. I think I know God in this moment—the poem in full attention, the attention like a priest at the altar with his belief and disbelief. I am cramped up with joy. I feel full with the great anticipation of holy light. Then, as if a metaphor in the eyes of the Lord, a tug and then another tug! The gofer is God, I think! Take the entire motherfucking thing! And, as not as if a soul in the world the weed is pulled into the earth and the device of poetry explodes.

Bulletproof

Love Song for the Makers I

This is a love song. They write like lepers of geometry.
Graph your own body like the Man. The peasants have
been etched by the sun. I read their eyes and see the
kings. My friend, write like the plague their beautiful
marks to take you to the kingdom. I hate them with my
peasant soul, etched by the dust, my hands dripping with
future, my soul as poor as the crown jewels. But they do
not know what a king means, the lepers, dead morsels of
code, fucked by their cash, stuffed like the olive eyes of
their treachery. I can see, when I look in their eyes, tables
full of other promises: death, punctual as the genetic code
they cannot touch. Hence my knife, my knife, from the
table of their making, stolen at the last instant when Jesus
is supposed to be over. Peasant that I am, I could use it to
make one point: look into the North Star and see how my
fake direction is absolute. I have closed my peasant eyes
and I am king and the knife is at the throat of God.

Love Song for the Makers II

This is the second love song: did I say lure? Of course I am not a fool. No love is a lure. No, love is the pith or pit of hate with your back against the wall. The crowning achievement of purity is to fathom impure. Hence hate, my friend, with his back against hers and she, my love, against the wall, turns to the north and I fall to the earth like milk, and am a fool to think I can save her. So I have nothing. I give in to hate because I cannot love, fool that I am, lost in the turn of her loss, lost in the hate that is lost. Lost that I cannot stop hating. I fall like milk upon the table, my tears white as my fury, the wall I am up against the absolute meaninglessness of love. Fathom this: you have hated your entire life and you fall, white against the dark, into your terror. Who will save you? You have lost everything. You are foolish as a name that you cannot pronounce. Rum. Fuck. Gazebo. Never. Nothing…She, with your cup of doubt in her eyes drinks your loss. You are alone in the womb, in her womb. Sudden as your loss.

Apollo Trade

I wanted to say that I am drowning. The worst of it was when the sun took it for me, brilliant, resplendent, took the ocean in her eyes, my sun, dear as the first vision of my birth. I was in the kingdom. I was gold. The repose of my act of being, worth to me more than nothing I can mention, struck by the fall, struck so deep I became the sun. Is life, I ask, the reflection of beauty? I could not breathe; the sudden thought that the ocean was my birth. How, in a trillion years, do we know each other? I looked deep into the water. It was gold. It was the unworn jewelry of my eyes. I wanted everything. When I conceived I dropped everything I knew, I became the water, and I did not perceive my drowning when Apollo dove deep into my art.

Pixel Chick

I don't care about the woman next to me on her computer,
in her computer…of. I care about how she was cloned, the
Petri Egg Vat of Nascence, her religion. She, in the system,
a pixel push, a perfect electrical fuzz of life. Since I cannot
love her, I see her shimmering like an oasis of love, yet
not love, more a fix to fit the programs of life. Alien. How
long has she had soul? How many dicks have fit her with
worm. How many lives has she saved in her making?
Since I cannot eye her yet she has eyes that flux modern
therapy into her box, I look at her like a star, one that has
imploded in space and watch the egg of her pulse with the
most attentive power. Nothing is stranger.

Virtues of Fantasy

The real world is not as strong as fantasy because fantasy is real and reality false. I could not say this for a long while. Now that I know, I feel the holes, the slips, the difference, and I long for the purple and silver light of a plumark. It is tiring living in-between. Having nowhere to go, I am in passage when the wind shifts the current, the seeds popping open elsewhere. When you know you are only barely there. When you forget everything, you are getting near. Yet, when the signs converge and you plummet into the signature of flow, your chances are very great. In and through. Dark patches of glow. Wet succulents of water pat on the refulgent floor of speech. Here you become whole, the full body of moths a-pulse with promise. Clearer than the moth or mouth in air your complete soul squeezes into the mark and time is edible. I pick seconds off the clock in green. Minutes of blue elongate and plume out like water. Marks of spirit shiver and percolate in the sails. We go deep the dip our on into the now and wellspring out into floral rivers. I am at home here. This is my world. This is where I want to live.

Confessions of Terms

I was sure of one thing: I would love on my own terms and
my own terms would live on me. I never questioned this.
I never doubted that this was the truth. What I doubted
was that I would forget to live or forget to know, or to
know how to live with forgetfulness. How many layers
of trust before the core? I was sure of one thing: the core
was absolute; the core was absolute trust…which meant
nothing until I, without question, lost all. Then, while I
shed my possessions and shucked my words, and the
slew of doubt that was my heart was beaten with the
gravitas of my desire, I became tempered like a sword,
sharp and defined as my wit, full with the fury of my deep
understanding of time. When, I learned, time becomes
or unbecomes, its edge is finite and pure. From this core
I pulled time, from my heart the blood of the edge of
the finite, and gave it to the sun. Everything burned, yet
purely, in the center of my heart. Sun resplendent! Sun
absolute! Sun pure as the edge of ice. Then, from my terms
I drew the law: I would live on my own terms and my own
terms on my own would live.

Nature Flower

Before, before I would get nervous, before the flower,
scintillating as life, refined in a cup of forever, perverse
dreams of light lambent in the bird bath, of soul and sex
and breaking, I would open and hurt into it. No mind was
my god. I followed where trust was least to find trust. I
did not know the words were petals, each one pulled up in
the seam of my night, closing, closing, closing my soul to
terror. When the night took me foolishly in, I did not know
the stars opened time and lay their voices into my stamen,
my bell, my thimble that stitched my consciousness like a
god-awful truth. Then silence. A vast sea plummeted into
my eyes. I knew then that words could do nothing alone.
I was shattered. I felt only the rush of one line of light
against my back, purely. In this moment I was the king
of nature. Why, I asked, could ink be so much a well and
waterfall? Why was the sum of my being made by a pen?
How much is all that blackness above an answer?

Loose

The music is off. I am drawn like a Ready Teller. Sip the bills back and watch the ink spread over in rainbows. Flutter of the film. Free of the draft, overdrawn and done. On nothing. Clear. Clear as the solvent in the throat of sex witches…they have only so much ass. As full as a factory in a sweatshop, trouble brews its own drink. Let them have it! I deep with the tea of exact measures. Perfect. Kill not and flow with the times. No one knows! I am happy to make them cakewalk the gallows. Why not? Because they invade my body of song. Without rhythm without love. Without knowing how to love. Take these lines to the beautiful hall and think your wake. I am tired of the spells. Trance dance future at the bank. And turn off the face of Ecila, Easy as law. Easy as full fools in the make jake the disaster by blowing out the candle with atomic love.

For the Prince

Re-alight yourself with the moon. Milk is my mother. Mother of god save the milk! The moon is milky. The words for the moon are black, night's river of surround sound. Open the ink and you get night. Kink open the milk and you get sun. All women know this. Out of the million ways to look at the moon you are one. You, white, milky, surrounded by ink. The sentence of darkness around such majesty is absolute. If your eyes go awry the sentence is cloud. Read through the veil to your bride, she looks like ash. Still, the embers, the stars, crinkle in the veil. Look again and she is not there. Use the stars to see your queen. If you see her face only she will be a wolf. If you know the sequence of the stars she appears, casts off her veil and, human, in the absolute of marriage, life, and love, you defy death. Make out with the moon for your water. Space has been waiting for centuries for the tremble of tremendous gratitude of the wind in your eyes.

Bulletproof

I am not looking for a woman. It is twilight. I am
uncentered from looking for a woman. Freedom has
always been sex. Sex has always been a chain. I am sham
shackled to the concept that no man needs to love when
there is a possession. Hence my luck who is male and my
encouragement who is this page. Could we meet in the
center? You be the woman. You be the concept. You be the
possession. And I will be the stripped down, threadbare
luck of this ink. I can see your eyes. They are hesitant; you
keep moving worlds with your desire. I am impure as
the history in your eyes, my own, and this earth's. Read
as deep as the world you are looking for. She is tempered
with pure hate. She is as deadly as her want. Like a game
of Russian roulette, the barrel turns. What world will love
you until you are bulletproof?

Confession Purification

Nothing is secret. I had the knowledge to give everything away. I was attacked. The psychical force was against my way. All I could do was read. I used every word to counter the sickness. It was the hardest thing I ever did. Every word like a rainstorm. They went dark and leveled me. Voices coming in like a blitzkrieg. My will, up against the wall, shook with measured fury. I had no thought of capitulation. All I thought was that I would blast through with every ounce of my strength. When I reached the center everything stilled. The light became nice. I felt warmth and relief and purpose. Yet up until this I fought with all my might against a demon horde of words that made me steel down to my quick. I didn't want to do this. I wanted my innocence. I wanted my love. Knowing that I had to fight, I burned their words in my repose. The years passed. Then, finally, when I had acted with every means I possessed, I rested. I could do no more. The feeling was very tiring, very bitter, and even deadly.

Definition of Black

Hot sun splurging on my table. Blitz of honey, cool as king inputs a love word. If every word were without connection then every correspondence would be cool, incompact, free of the hinge of speech. Connect me to the sun and the world will cool over in tides of deep meaning. I am unsure. My pen drops rivulets of rhythm in this heat. Read the sunspots on the page as magnetic. Pull from their draw your purity. Black is the meaning of life. How many times do I read this and cure into your sure ecstasies of nothing. The universe is about to turn into the opposite of its meaning. You be black and pure. They will be white and read. On the edge of the universe is a black hole. The center is brilliance. Turn the center right and you are the truth. And in the center of the truth is a sun, new and brilliant as the pure form of love. I am your driver to the system. Call yourself the mean of this myth and fall up into the pool of this form and cleanse yourself. We are men. We are to the stars men. We mean are light is blackness.

Reich Deposition

48° 45 N. 0° 10 E.

Goebbels

Behind the cigarette, the simple state
Spiraling twitchy with reflections of Jews,
Snake eyes slick amok the diamond of history,
The turn now Normandie's, is a sentence…
"My dear invaders, you see I am the news
Rapt with audience purity, the word
Soaks in the assault on shoreline, I,
As always, roar in laughter at your thought
That you will see me through. Nothing sticks
To the eyelash of truth, that power will sink
To the depths of my root and clear me. I am…
 After all, the music that everybody fell for." In the pith
Of his cocked tongue he feels…"They say that
The Allies will pour through the front lines in
Sincere form, like Marks in a gypsy's hand,
But they cannot pay me to death. I sweat
Only the multiplicity of bad puns in my writers,
Bunkered up here like a box from Egypt. Time
Evens me up with my medicine so I don't lose the whole.
My plans (you see it here), sculpt sure
The contour of vision. And I am not
The absence, but the entirety of time,
Like brother Rommel in the desert,
Our footprint of lion, Sphinx-poised,
Eternal, occult-sweet, reflecting in cross.
My cyanide and my Luger, the cocked sure
Feeling of multiple deaths abstract, I,

Goebbels! Architect of the German Uber Stadt!
Ever vain of Reich power, exist! Outside
The reports are sporadic. My wife sits with
Her legs spread, picking sex blood
From her hair. My gun is precariously balanced in a bible.
I remember my vows and infinity blessings. This will not end,
I muse, with one war. This the beginning.

Spawn

Hitler's forty-six offspring do not know who they are.
One death nurse for each whelp. They tend the tyrants
In forty-six different countries. The nurses
Are trained to teach each magic trick. The lies
Are sure to claw open at a certain point
And swear down the root of the next century,
Real as every wonky surreal.
Pop! And these worm empty out, like seeds
A fire, meaning a-pulse in slurry death
Of previous assaults, plumbing memory
For the secret loops all powerful with fake
Architecture. Spool out and within the spawn
Law absurd! Then, like truth, but not, they take
Their seats afire with life act of hell.
It took Hitler one thousand nights of copulation
To get his boys. Goebbels did it in a straight forty-six.
Himmler was barren and killed his tricks.
Rommel was greedy and had seventy. Himmler
Struggled with gay issues. But in the end a
Solid Aryan pack of two hundred and eight
Demons to continue the race. This means
Two hundred and eight death nurses, all of which
Tick hide in the social skin, screwed in for fuck all time
With their kid fit to enter institutions for profit.
Each would, of course, teach the child occult matters
Of high Reich way. The boys would think in church
Of all the good they could do. God will

Grant us our life!...As he does always.
Then into business and politics.
Who would know the cryptic tease in their heads?
Mini Fuhrers who would plant every act,
Their reflective learning of horror…
Two hundred and eight chances to subvert
The major nations! For what? For the black queens.
The vision of the future. For death song.

Fuhrer

Hope was the lack of art that was not Hitler's strong point.
The Allies have painted the Mulberry Harbors red!
Parachuters everywhere, like
Lemmings. In war silence he gazes
Upon his stock, the multiple couplings with other
Women to preserve the race funny, his Uber plan
Punctured like molar rot. The air in the room is
Dank. The chocolate lined up for the children.
The maps burned. The last Jew ready to prophesy
In the fires. "I feel sad that I will not meet
Churchill in the commons, or on the moors
With a gun. We could have ended it that way—
Proper as the decimation of my million
Souls. I will listen to radio and look at reports.
The entire channel full with those pasty white
Roast Beef! I am the champion of the new world!
My melancholy is poetry! My spirit is the ash
Of Jew graves! How will I look with a bullet
Bursting through my temple, blood and bone red splattered
Into the wall? Beckman beautiful…Picasso smart.
I want to be filmed. I want it
To last forever on an American reel! Put it
In the eyes of all those heathen children! I want it
To roast in the frontal lobe of Roosevelt until
His wheelchair roll is battery powered.
It is silent. The room is perfect.
I have gotten a belly from all those nice meats.

I am looking in the mirror…All I wanted was to
Be an artist. Now death, the finest art project of all!…Ya
I could have painted the world with my blood.

Rommel

I am up the ass of Hitler for a botched job.
Always upp the ass of the Fuhrer. It wasn't
My fault. We didn't prophesy with the body's right.
I told him to read the crows feet we cut up
In Mussolini Olive Oil, not blood. I like my soldiers. The tanks
Are exciting when they explode. Luftwaffe
Are fantastic for children. When we were shut
Out by MacArthur I was on the turret looking
At the ass of an Egyptian Girl. Ya. I could have
Won. I hated Hitler, his gold horde, the genetic
Engineering, the way he felt maps, his stoicism,
The risk he took going into France. I
Hated him because when I fucked him upp the ass
He extracted my cock and said it was a lizard.
We never got on after that.
Now in this bunker and my Luger isn't even
Greased. I'm going out fighting. Blow a hole
In my head, ha. I'll run right into this Doughboy
Fantasy on my ruin. We will bleed
Together. I, Rommel of the desert, once bitten
Vamp, Hitler bugger, boy leader. I will suck
My final cock and then blast a hole in the
Special forces front man so we go together.
It will be like my ejaculation into the cumquat
Turdhind of Hitler. I will absorb the bullet. It will
Be in my memory of Poland, the first betrayal
In the theater. I will be naked, Teutonic, and real.

Lattarice Aroshel glint lights with the direct mark,
Pulls into the channel of the General's thought
Figuring into "once bitten vamp", and then curls
On the curvature of "Hitler", skipping to "absorb"
And at "bullet" plunges "I will" in her turn of storm
"In my memory" to steel (in-to "ki-ss") open "theater"
Shifts, flash art I call edge to the throat…"naked" in the
"Teutonic Real"…slices the chords of breath from his words…
I, Lattarice Aroshel of storm, demand your soul!
The room quivers and History fixes the depth
Of the blade in Rommel, forever.

Himmler

Looking into the twilight, Himmler's cross
Glints as if a film in tide-pool, where his mind
Reruns again and again, Jesus-hooked and
Impossible as escape. He pitches. "I,
Hung up in this bunker, the scent of Hitler's
Tense return, Goering's map sweat, Goebbels ink to
Communicate the disaster…sink. I feel like a leaf
Looping in the air, dizzy as the yessing "Zero
Zoo" infatuation dame school! Turn this around? GI
Unstrung on beach. I, the essence of a pool.
Beautiful, beautiful. The Roast Beef cracking our safe…
Will the bullet really be silver? Silver as will
Really bullets be? Return the times I
Have communed with vamps, Ya my pulse sweet,
Blood sucking vamps. A religion of
Indubitable emptiness. My allegiance to the vein…
And nobody will know, my stocking around the
Paris palaces in my briefs howling like a wolf.
We must play. There is no other way to relieve
The stress. All that fighting and then what…who
Could deny a taste of our occult matters? When
The Royal Marines break down the door my candles
Will be lit, my sacrificed lamb drunk, my Luger
Barrel hot with my self-made end note that I
Have named "Genie". Bang! And then what? Do I
Believe in God? Really? I have only succumbed to
The cock of my Fuhrer. What after? Snake charming?

They will put my body in a museum and the children may see
My tattoo, "Skin Flick". But God…if he does exist, I
Will kill him and start a franchise in Heaven.
Himmler folds his ego and in the crease
Is surged out of flux by reflection. "I am…I",
Yet Farina pulses blue in her music, turns
Him to face and her edge sleek light plunges answer…
Whispering deep desert words she settles the edge
Of Fremen promise in a turn like a tide.
Off sung his throat screams silently blue,
Cutting the dream of war with particular care…
Himmler slumps to this absolute truth: justice
Will answer all horror exact…we are the song of
Dune, unbound and pure in our fate.

Sword

The mist is a song. Do not think you are not
Stronger than the mettle of your way. The subject
Is sensitive as a kiss. When you descend
Into the bunker you are the mist, Aroshel
Lattarice. Your edge sharp with salt water. The hum
Drinks from the skies the landing song of the
Channel. Everything is calm. There is a
Slight tinge to the darkness. Fai'y shiver.
Channel scent. Pith of the night. The Blitz
On the beachhead exclaims light below.
You curl into the dive like an autumn leaf.
From your guts the direction of the play.
Lattarice flows the milk devout of attack.
Light on the blade of Aroshel like a
Candle. You point down into the job
Splintering music meaning. The pulse of
Meaning bursting outward and around. From
Your lips the decent direct channel into
The bunker. Through like a wraith, the
Startling face of Goebbels is hewn. Lattarice
Turns in blade verse. Song wraps around his
Throat, The blade work of the dark and
Popping lights in a circle. Struck deep his
Throat opens in a scream. The news of
Five years spills red on his coat. You
Pull the blade back and his head tilts
And falls. A great darkness, like ink spills.

Your song finishes with the final answer
Of death…Jew answer…the steel ice hot,
Hotter than the fires.

Juno

I used to play a violin but now I play machine gun.
What poetry there is in the pen of a bullet! I have lined
Up the chefs against the stove. The only witness
Will be the meat. We are negotiating for seconds…
How funny it all is…the war…the deaths. If
Only Churchill knew my most intimate thoughts.
He would see me in a pram with a lollipop bomb.
I would see his jowls puff smoke from his
Tobacco chops. We could have been friends,
Bunk mates and cricket hitters. Now just these
Destitute cooks…they burned the sausage and
Overcooked the potatoes. If I am going to go the
Whole fucking staff will, too. Negotiating for seconds…
Ha, the fools! In ten minutes the door will crack. Churchill
And I, we could have tossed
The rugby ball back and forth. I will tell
Him how to lay mines with champagne,
He would discuss Carthage and Rome. Can a mind
Summon one's fate? If I imagine Churchill as a cook will
I truly kill the Minister? Fucking cooks, they
Have got ten seconds off me. Churchill in my head
Like a Shepherd's Pie. I cannot shake him…
I am shaking. His cheeks puff one last cloud over me:
"Eichmann, Eichmann! Do you see my field revolver?
I am pointing the muzzle at your German Cross. I am a real
Dream with a bullet! If you think trigger you will click
Your heals and enter Heaven." Fuck Churchill.

But he's right; the trigger is God, a bi-polar swinging
Deity for all. "Eichmann, did you know that the imagination
Designs destiny!" God damn you Churchill, I'm going to
Pop your fat cheeks so your cigar penetrates your brain!
"There you Kraut muttering mad man…look at my thought…"
Eichmann drops to the ground, a puppet show bow,
Crumpled into Winston's idea of lead.

Gold

I am loaded like pistons in the push. Ya…
I protect the liberties of the Reich…Ya…
Free German. Free Uber Stadt. Free Kraut.
I am loaded like my cards are loaded:
Ace liquor, fine whisky, cure-all champion
Champagne to fuck up the ebullience of assault. Stout
British Sten to Pop Tart the beef. I am loaded
On Gaverte Strategy number Mein Kampf.
God damn tippling Luger fuck! I will spill
Out only most savory bullet throw-up. Swine
Roast Beef. Let them come and I will suck
Back the last bottle of blitz barrel one
Thousand and two and pop them English
With my load. Load? Yes…was ist dis
Wonder chill of ignorance…? "I am loaded"
Slinkwell a-tunes "liberties of the Reich"
"Number Mein Kampf" "savory" "blitz"
"Caves" in "my massacre" "buffing the spume"
Curves deep into the "Fat cow chugger"
"Bullet beast", and into the marks, like…"Howitzer cock"…
Bursting over the seamen! They will eat my
Muzzle blaze, bullet beast that she is.
I am more loaded than the boats that
Cave my massacre into zipping cream puff
Points in my Howitzer cock buffing the spume
In squirrels on these heathen. There, I said it.
My hand is on the…hiccup…trigger…hiccup…the

Blam! Hiccup, God save the Fuhrer. God
Save the hiccup, blam! Fucking Doughboy!
Bastards. I will stutter their blood
Across the walls and sing…BLAM!

Utah

"Ludwig fucking Beethoven…we've got him.
Wolfgang fucking Mozart…Wilhelm fucking Richard Wagner…
Johann Fucking Bach…Goddamn
Friedrich fucking Baumfeld…Jean fucking
Berger…Johannes fucking Brahms, and
The beginning of the English Language…and still we
Can't hold a Goddamn beachhead! Ah, the turntable
Of life! Circular Geists are storming my signs.
The needle is the fog light. Play back the crystal
Nodes of my dreams. Scratch in the vinyl
The sound for the times. I turn and empty.
I empty and turn. Surrounded by life! War life!"
The needle skips and the gap in the composers
Opens up the whole….Through the mist
The note of a blade. Aroshel Lattarice turns
On the pitch of her edge. "Pour oil on all
Of them Britch Roast Beefs! Grind them
Into shoreline mud! Bulldoze their history
In their eyes with German Uber Stadt!" In
The contour of the language Aroshel, figuring,
Illumines "pour" and slips into "shoreline",
Flutters on "history in their eyes", and then plunges
Into "Stadt"…"But it is no use my Fuhrer.
They have broken the bunker door!
They are storming down the hall! You must…
Escape or die!" Click. Blam! "Enough with you,

Servant. This is my glory. I am going to the devil…"
Rivulets of voice, Aroshel falls into "use",
Interpreting "broken", turns to "door",
Fulfilling "storming down", curves into "must"…
"I will sit at my seat with my bible and then,
When they turn the knob, I will pull
The trigger and blow infamy into their line.
Bastard English! They will not trouble my last minute with
Pansy actions. Let them see my moment
As the lofty rampart gaze into their lack.
Churning into "infamy", to "see my moment",
The blade "lofty" "into their lack" sings…
"All Royal Marines into my divorce
From their clutch-hungry tea totaling hands.
There. The Flight of the Valkyries. I will add
My crescendo. Less than a minute. Ten,
Nine, eight, seven…one click! NO! A jammed
Bullet! The knob! I am fucked!

Point Du Hoc

The fog—such a British bard—hugs the coast.
Seamen come up the beach in furtive waves.
I am looking down the barrel of a Howitzer,
My dear, waiting to put a puncture into the prow
Of the cordite fire spitting ships. My eye,
If you must know, was donated by a black
Wraith. "You'll see God more than once a day,
Sir!" I, however, cannot see a thing! I will
Tend to the witchdoctor later for my gaze.
In the crack of the bunker, I, Goering. More
Famous than the Spam advertisements on tongues!
If it is the crack of my skull that tends
The gun, I will fire it with my neurons
And feel the Serotonin elate the harbor. Suddenly
Shrieking from the air…a new radio instrument
To destroy our field? We are nameless the fog
Holds. Feeling into "witchdoctor", I "crack
The bunker" slips to "famous", curl back "on tongues",
Deeps into "skull that tends the gun" "fire" felt,
Whips back "neurons", and dives into "Serotonin"
"Ships" "My Dear" "waiting" "my eye" and turns
Goering illuminated by a cigarette…
A black shadow shrieks in with blade….
"The harbor" floods, "suddenly shrieking",
Opens "from the air" into "radio instrument",
Trues the "field" and "we are nameless" in depth.

The smile on Goering's neck slits. Blood hot
The shrill cry gurgles. But there are always
Last thoughts for tyrants…."All I felt was
The curvature of my sex…and then blackness
Darker than my idea of love." The pulse
In the darkness slumps the body down. The clink of the Iron
Cross on cement. Vacant eyes curl back the pitch honesty of
fate.

Omaha

In a memory loop, Hitler intuits the feel and the shot in
His brain matter blitzed red on the wall…watches his
Thought ricochet back into brain and out
The other side…ricochet
Off his silver coffee cup and back through his eye…off
Ricochet to his bone and punch in a brilliant splurt ricochet
Of brain… Ricochet off the Luger handle and burst through (of
His right ventricle)…Ricochet off of the hilt his
Sword and blow out the cerebral cortex…Ricochet sword
Out and into his German Cross and blow out
His right eye…I, Aroshel Lattarice, the "hilt"
And "bone" of truth my "cup", at the "handle" "burst"
Out "into his German Cross" "horror" "broken"
And "blitz" "liver" off the back "Language Center",
"His right eye" of "Monocle" and "mirror", his
Ricochet of "spirit" un-arted and void, ricochet
Off the box of maps and ricochet off
On through his jaw…Ricochet off of his molar blow on
Off life and explode against his sinuses…filling off
Ricochet out and off the mirror frame and plummet ricochet
Back through his coccyx…blow out his hip and back
Ricochet off the pile of pocket change and reenter his ricochet
Left eyeball…blow out the Language Center and left
Ricochet off of the monocle chain…back into ricochet
And through his stomach…tear out the other side and
Ricochet out off of the back of his gilt chair ricochet
Slam into his liver and bust out his colon…slam!

Ricochet off the door handle and blitz in to ricochet
His bloody crotch in blood blow…out the tip of his cock his
Lodge and death bunker of fate, Lodge forever eternal, lodge
Deep in his Language Center splintering out voices…deep.
Ah, mein Fuhrer…the horror...

Flux Documentation

Channel Crossing (Normandy, June 6, 1944)

I wrote Flux initially at the French Press Café in one stream, by hand and unknowing of its magnitude. When I returned home I read it and wept, for it described not only my trial over the past seven years, but also it had, imbedded within, my grandfather's trial at D-Day. I could see in the handwriting sentences that were not my own. Some of the sentences were very focused handwriting. So, within the actual writing was a cryptic translation of both profound and normal insight. What I observed was that the cryptic words were Fairy writing. I read the piece maybe ten times and I did not doubt that it was a special message written for me…from "somewhere else" and my initial feeling was very emotional and pithy as if a spirit was rising in my guts, a spirit that was completely fortified by the act of the poetry. I wondered what it was and realized that the spirit was my grandfather's. Hence the title.

Symbolically, the channel was literal and figurative. I was receiving a "channel" about the Channel. The gravitas of this date also struck me. I could "see" Angels and Fairies fighting for England and the messages they carried were vital. There was a strategy in the images, and the voices in my heart, in my grandfather's heart, were all the "voices" in the "crossing". In this way this first poem proved to me that magic exists, that fantastic beings exist and that I was from this line. My hate…in love… "lived" a valid existence. I could, from here, speak of and for the gravest time in my family's history

My acceptance of the Fairy voice was a prime act of mythos meeting real. Fairy means, "to speak". All I had wanted during my trial was to speak. Hence this poem…the

most ultimate trial and time was my rite. That the emotional
tenor was described, of the landing at Normandy, was my
attack upon the horror of the Nazi/terror problem in psychical
time and space. By accepting my hate/love I gave myself the
right to "kill". By eradicating the fear I awoke into my own
kingdom…that of pure Fairy language. This, for me, was the
most profound poem I have ever written. I cannot say enough
of the depth. Even this sentence is wrong. I must say enough
to survive. Yet, from this first poem I knew that I had entered
an important new space, poetically, spiritually, mythically, and
sovereign. As it was written by hand but was an important
message means that I had "received" the poem and was
informed of my struggle, my path, my rite, and my freedom…
to speak in the channel for my life and the life of my family,
from somewhere else.

The Kingdom

Writing blindly, my flow a pouring of language out (with hardly a mistake, and no critical stops), my language unimpeded and thus pure since I did not check my pen, this poem produced itself. I see, after reading, that this is a medical poem, the declaration of "I feel ill" if observed on the page in line with the body's liver and surrounding it the brilliant green light of pure columns or architecture. There is also a repetition in "Flux" of nothing, the purity of not, or the space where everything flows into. Here it is in "feelings un-rupture..." and "nowhere greens out in striations..." Thus the kingdom is in "nowhere", full of green light and is empty and force "in-between" that stitches feelings. Most ultimately, in my opinion, the kingdom or feeling of kingdom is emotion/feeling...an intense engagement with the viscera. When "in no time I answer" the double entendre shows that also there is "no time" in the kingdom a place full of fluid, light, and mistakes. The declaration that "we are ink" suggests you can get to the kingdom by becoming a book or ink or reading...As for "we survive in the mistake..."it is evident to me that when there is a mistake in a perfect universe there must be a lesson or a perfection in the mistake revealing something else. That I see this as a medical poem having placed myself as an ill person in the center right means that I am trying to heal myself...which I was at the time. The fact that Flux is full of "commas" is that co-ma or calm awe are natural desires. And then in the center of the poem there is the question "how long has it been since you have felt your home." This is a question of inside and outside, meaning I am, as a writer, "outside" my work. The question begs the desire to be "in" the kingdom. And, that there is something "else" to the kingdom depicts that the writing is an act of going somewhere to get home. Hence the kingdom is a place of green light that is helping, that is elsewhere, that is empty, full of language, nowhere and a mistake that is full of columns where books and light turn around and is fluid or full of fluid where one may become healthy. That the kingdom is placed in text or medium is declaring that the kingdom either uses or implements itself in language and that by reading certain poetry we may transcend or acquire the flow of green light that is nowhere yet all present in the mélange. To feel this medium is the profound feeling of transference of a power that poetically is the vital we need to survive, communicate, and to, most importantly, feel. Hence the right reading is essential to procure the ecstatic effect of now, presence, completeness, and ultimately love. My desire to build this feeling is motivated by my innate draw to speak, hear, and sense life in the rapture of art.

Practical Matters of Royalty

Without a guard the king is helpless. The first thing a king should do upon coronation is to knight his men. Yet in this poem the channel has been crossed, the kingdom has been described, the Normandy landing is ever present, so knighting is necessary. That the men are unseen is the admission of an "invisible" entourage. The play from "knights" disappearing in the day where "angels" appear in the "light" is the idea that a reinforced support of knight to angel and heavenly interaction supports the myth occurring here. Yet the most important thing is that the writer appears as a metaphor where his entire consort passes through. Metaphor means literally to "bear across". After the angels, Fairy, knights, elves pass then the confirmation that where from these words come are gold is the special marking of a True King. Indeed he says, "I speak the truth". This makes the metaphor statement profound…because as a metaphor his is the "gate", "bridge", the "door". And since the truth is the center of the king, all entrances are "true" or pure. The acknowledgement that there is "no god" gives the king the ultimate act…for if there is no God, the king is the ultimate figure. And that Language is king means all passes through the language and speech crowns the innocent with life. This at most is the acknowledgement that language makes kings, who are the door and give life.

Interpretation of Narnia

I admit that I must be under a spell, which I call here Narnia. This is an ever-present story in my childhood. I think that "when I awake there will be a reverse of Narnia." The way I interpret the world is backwards, hence I spell Narnia backwards. I also admit my priest, who I might be, and who thinks the world is on the brink. This being true moves the action forward. I substitute Aslan for the myth of Androcles and the Lion. I want to heal Aslan who stands for Christ and whom the White Witch wants to sacrifice. Edmond, beguiled by the White Witch, acts as Androcles and pulls the thorn from Aslan's paw. I say that this act preempted the cru-ci-fiction because I wanted to save Christ. Again, here a metaphor is bearing across that undermines the White Witch, as Aslan is the lion and Edmond is Androcles. The "repayment" is my revenge for the witch fucking up the story and, indeed, Aslan then will save Edmund later…in battle. The multiple reversals and the loyalty regained by the myth changes the fate of Aslan, Edmond, and Narnia. Hence Narnia can win and Christ may not be sacrificed. The metaphor is the time machine that allows for the switch to ameliorate. Since myth and reality are always makers of the other I rewrite the myth to correct the divine problem.

Aroshel & Lattarice

When reality fails one turns to fantasy for the solution. Reality has failed me so I have given birth to the real myth of Aroshel and Lattarice, my sword. Losing reality I have lost my belief in my identity. Thus my identity is everybody else. To redefine who I am I have fought. My swords were thus created. She has not been held in eleven years. I am tired of fighting yet I want to end their existence. Who are they? Everybody who gets in the way of my art. I have multiple attributes. My sword is one of my attributes. Then I show how it is art. One evening I put it in O'rien's sheath. I actually felt it symmetrically placed. So now I am looking for my sword. Hide in plain sight. Again I use the metaphor to hide to reveal her. It is a slip in time…a fold that is reproductive. I admit my talent with metaphors. Aroshel Lattarice is here…but hidden. I think of what makes a sword— fire, metal (mettle). I admit it must be ice that has made my sword. I break down the metaphor and find I will find Aroshel in crystal. I am tired of wars. I address fantasy that is real (this is a true statement) and find that she is in the ocean…the queen of the world. I interchange the myth of Arthur in Cornwall with my grandfather who names her Sally. He throws her into the sea…a direction I must go. His muse is the sword. There is an abstract message of killing. Sally or Aroshel is Charlie (fool) and Lattarice is the Fairy name for Gabriel (angel). My grandfather has killed but is forgiven. I reverse the blade to "L'eshora", the name of the body that the ocean beats. I am sure. This lies before me in blue pools.

Sword Documentation

I am trying to find my sword. It is hard making a myth that is real. I note that time has been broken, an event largely punctuated by the Industrial Revolution and technology. In the gap of time there is a lake (I see this as a metaphor). In the lake all are held in reflection (judgment etc.). I note that the sword might be here and then link it to Excalibur. I admit I have the mark of the cup. And this is the Holy Grail/sword. I admit that the sword is a phallus. This is true. But in the lake is one reflection. With the right recipe the reflection, this reflection will spill like a lake. I admit my archetype…that I know this historically. So now I know the future or my path to the sword/grail/phallus. An individual will, at the right time, draw Aroshel from the abyss…meaning "draw" to make a drawing (artfully). I include a random notation about the Pope's name as Simplicimus from Grimmelshausen…the destiny of the Pope. At the right reflection the song (reflection) will make the lake or (reflection) into a sword. Here time that is broken will be drawn together and there will be a great battle for truth.

This is both the sword documentation and the fate of the actions in time.

"To Bring Them To Bear"

Hence the necessity of sin(g) king into your own truth…that you can hold and demand the universal scale or (justice). Then go to the queen (ocean) and read your soul in her reflection (lake). Do not conjure for conjuring is fake and weak…you must demand the ocean (queen) to procure Aroshel. If you are true to the queen then your voice will raise her…your sword. If you draw Aroshel then you will either be slain or forgiven…the danger of magic and sex and truth together. If you are true then you will possess the right song. Your song may be fearful, doubtful, or lovely and still it will if true procure the blade. Aroshel will bury herself in your truth…meaning perhaps that the female will have sex with you in reverse…her phallus in your cup. This understanding is the gift. Open now your voice Fairy. One must rest after for one day. Then wait for O'rien the hunter and take/withdrawal from his belt your Selinquel (the name of Aroshel Lattarice at night). You will know the truth. Then go to the ocean/queen and say the right words for Lattarice. Your emotion will be your guide and answer. You will be purified. Release yourself. Your intuitive action will weld Lattarice Aroshel. Then, from yourself, draw both edges.

Milk Cure

The authentic moon to open this passage is to acknowledge that there is a fake moon. This milk cures the edge of Aroshel. The milk is a story. The story insinuates birth milk or the vitality of life. The story glows white around the blade of Lattarice. The changing of names is phonic. I.e. Lattarice "slinks well". Selinquel is a story and tells her sharp story to the word. Hence stories speak both in words and to words. Selinquel is the answer to the demons that visited me from the third world. Then Aroshel reverses after the foundry to L'eshora. The milk or story is, in daylight, pure song, that turns or uses verse in the feel of the light. Story in the milk metaphor cures reality so that it is as real and falseness that is fake. "My friends do not want to change." I.e. The statement, out of place, shows that there is, between worlds, one side that is too reasonable. My sword cures both worlds, the demonic world and the real. To cure the demons one must verse turn the song and the moon or milk will answer. This is sight in darkness. For the Fairy the song of the sword is its trust. I say I cannot see any of the work, which means I have the trust of no sight or purity. Therefore I am of sword. All swords names turn meaning: Selinquel, Aroshel, Lattarice…they are exact.

A Dream Battle

As I unwound this story, fluxing from rehab at Vista Del Mar, in the café where from I flowed ink as if a storm I realized I was fighting for the myth of my life. The most blatant truth was that I had failed…I couldn't write against the storm within. So I wrote the storm of my myth in a battle of dream. As I emptied upon the page my poetry, up against the most mammoth perception…for what could be more mammoth than my recognition! Slowly I pressed into the wall, against the horror of my visions. Short, staccato sentences, direct poetic, almost raging in the absolute that I must fight. All of the horror of the universe bore down upon me. Then symbols: cold stone (castle, my blade in the stone, the song coming forth. I was alone…I had banished my family to save them. My song faltered. Blind against a leviathan. And then at the utmost loss my steel in my right hand. The light in my hand ready. The bitter, bitter realization of a battle and I strike and brilliant light that is blinding pressing into the edge. I, innocent, am aware of light only and the admittance that my spirit is terrible. This is an absolute test, for my sword is writing an imagination that does not fail me. In this way I learned some of the power of Lattarice Aroshel.

Mirror School

The event of this poem was hallucinogenic in that in my mind
there was a reverse mirror that performed as my myth/reality
in attempt to "see" the real sword in my own body. To begin
with hating myself purely is to combine with hater purity,
a state of visceral emotion that is sharp, maybe even acidic.
Excalibur is the known sword of Arthur, which repeats in
comparison here because I am from the "Arthurian" line. Upon
saying that only a fool would name her is my way of saying
that I am a fool…the necessary assumption for this imagining.
Then I turn and am "leaved" by the forest (a pun). Then,
turning again…or versifying again, I am given a lake/reflection.
Upon turning a third time I am given the lake as a mirror…
which I was standing in in my house. I then meet the Lady of
the lake who I think is in the wrong place. I ask her to life up
my reflection to see what the nameless is (I can only assume
God). She holds my body still…I think I am the sword (absolute
empathy of my magic). I am the archetype of the sword
meaning the historical symbol. The edge of the sword is my
lips, i.e. what pronounces words. "They have stolen centuries"
signifies my lips have stolen time (poetic). Because of this
"everybody" coalesces into the mirror and I am burned with the
mark of the sword. I ask the lady to take her from me (a reversal
of Arthurian receiving Excalibur). The sword "mistakes" the
mirror for a lake. (I want the reflection). The lady, or the reader
"brings me up"—meaning "raises" me. I.e. my mother. The
air or heir takes me. I am song. I am tempered by the nature of
the song/sword/heir. I demand the absolute right/rite of my
nature. The words try to calm me. I am only held by the heir…
i.e. the sword only fits the right person. As if a

forge, I am struck hard and forged in memory…meaning as the heir I am deep within my memory and that may be a scar from the forge…my root. Memory is recalled and there is yellow light. History is England's and is freezing or "free sing". Yet the weather is my edge of my lips. This time the poem makes me pure. I see my sword/ song released in memory/reflection. I am the shape t. Truth is the final answer…the beauty of my reflection and sword.

Within this poem I have seen myself, sword, upside down. This was the test t. To see regularly in reverse to divine my sword/ person/spirit. This was a very visual/imaginative poem.

The Exchange of Lattarice for Farina
"Water Gift"

My blood and tongue are both English and Cockney. I look
and there is a lake I cannot view…the irony being I can see
something that isn't there. Cockney is a very musical language.
I close my eye that is blind and see music or the kingdom. It is
phosphorescence or FA for Essence…the fourth note Fa (as in
the Sound of Music). Endless light. The promise of Aroshel "in
verse" in a poem is as dream. I admit my fear to sing my mind.
The result is that my Cockney has drowned in the no music…I
speak softly. I admit that I am under the House of Atreides
spell…to trade. The Fremen know my spell is true. I compare
Aroshel to the Kris Knife…two different blades. The Fremen
or free men welcome my edge. For poetry they have given me
Kris Knife. The edge of the knife is blue/voice. You understand
the blade by how it speaks. I show Lattarice (sadness, tears)
and the Fremen give me for the water sacrifice the most loyal
gift. Farina is the blue edge trust…this is a prophecy of my
daughter's birth. Apollo makes Elvin light cure on Farina's
edge. I utter… "I son will be born," which is actually wrong
because Farina, my daughter, is "female". The birth has been a
natural wound. The gap in time is "cauterized,"…i.e. the lake
is cured by fire. My daughter's voice is at my neck. "Translate
your soul"…or know your truth. I show my eyes are also
Fremen. We are in agreement with my song. I am released by
Farina. In this rite I am in absolute loyalty with my daughter.
This is a prophecy.

The Instrument of Aroshel & Lattarice

I have been in both literal and figurative storms. Here I admit
that the figurative storm is the most difficult. The will is tested
in both. To be without action conceivable is to be blind. I put
Jesus Christ in the real storm because he seems always to
be a matter of fact to religion…yet also I remove him from
the fantastic or figurative so that he might be less problem
and more solvable in reality. And Buddha is placed in the
figurative—the most difficult—because Buddha represents the
utmost peace and balance. Then I make the figurative storm and
Aroshel rains. When Aroshel breaks she becomes Lattarice or
"the tears of sadness". Rain and sun. When after it rains Aroshel
is broken (the sun is broken) then, at that moment, the puddles
show Lattarice and when the sun comes out they fuse together
as one. This tells of how Aroshel is returned. Indeed, it tells of
how "L'eshora" may save Lattarice, or sadness. I lift from the
puddle, or the lake/reflection my sword with my eyes. I am
sure of its power. My eyes raise her green…my eyes are green.
When, ultimately, death or the west comes, Aroshel Lattarice,
one blade of sun and rain (the elements) will be drawn from
Apollo, God of poetry. This is how Apollo gives the voice or
Fairy the dark Elvin instrument of justice to the poets. I say
dark Elvin because of the balance of "dark and light".

The Jack Matter Section

This section is titled Jack Matter because I channeled Jack
Spicer to create these poems. It also refers to the Union Jack of
the United Kingdom, as the next section is, post landing upon
Normandy, referential to WWII. Although the section has very
little engagement with the Nazis it is an honest look into how
to live, who saved me, what wit is, how to love, how to avoid
sacrifice, and overall is clearly the volume of Spicer's sensibility.
The reason I know this is because once you have read Spicer
you can hear his voice distinctly and it is capable of poem.

I

The first poem tells me (as one should listen to the channel if it helps) of my loyalty of poetry and my muse. Upon slipping into the world of poetry I was given a choice: what do I bring to hell. I chose to bring poetry to hell in place of my love or a woman. This ultimate choice determines my ethics…saving a life comes before my craft. With this standard I have been in hell writing for some twenty-two years. Jack assuages me by noticing my sacrifice and by telling me that hell and heaven are distinct and un-crossable (possibly to save heaven) Jack tells me that after being in hell my muse is now in my words/mouth and I can hold her and trust by speaking.

II

It is appropriate to be blunt about life, or more direct;
this includes death. Hence I open this poem with two flat
statements...or rather Jack does. I state that death will never
conquer life. Then Jack enters and says that he is skeptical as
hell. Yet skepticism is the most necessary tool with which to
understand life and death. Jack admits that "they" (whoever
they are) poisoned him when he was drinking. Ironically as
he collapses in the elevator he is "rising". Practically at this
juncture he admits that it is a fact that life that we know both
lives and dies. This poem is my need to address the ultimate
for the sake of freedom of speech. I.e. if death makes us silent
then even though we live we are dead. Jack asks how could
he love the choice of death. Tristan's devotion to Isolde is
made present...to go to hell for love. And also Romeo's stupid
mistake of death. Jack iterates that he is alive (in undead form)
today because his sorrow could not kill. This pun is double
edged: could not kill him and could not kill another. All poets
are fraught with sorrow...it is a matter of existence if one feels.
Hence poison, the cup of sorrow we all must drink is only the
"idea" of death...but not death really. He is trying to explain
why I live. When Jack states that he "drowned his sorrow in
a cup" he means he drunk away the sorrow or reduced it in
his "liberty". Yet he doesn't mean beer or whisky...he means
he drunk his trust (life) and on this very slim sensibility he
awoke (although undead) all of his passions and looked out of
my eyes. In essence he gave me his cup of sorrow (trust) from
which I now write. In this manner he is writing me and I, too,
am his most cherished game...as he says, "you are my home
run."

III

I am recovering from my breakdown, my seven-day stay at Vista Del Mar Psych Ward, an unwinding jumble of energy and perception. This history behind me is intense, stuff I can't explain in contrast with reality. Whose reality? Don't we all have different realities? Then suddenly a man's eyes that are scales. I am writing without any restraint, there are very few mistakes; I am in some channel, in flow. My eyes are songs…FA for Essence. And I can fly with them. Where to? How many women know these songs? I am centered…a small drop of me in my heart. But I have not been here before (Jack is absent). I don't know the rules. (Roethke's line "My secrets cry aloud"). I am raw from my experience. I tell myself to be the sun ringing out in the pool. I question loyalty…drinking not my own blood. Yet I shun all alliance…even with myself, my trust thrust into the skepticism of the past. An unknown child shakes in the pool (refer to channel) my trust. I do not know how to advise him. All the shit of the world is impossible to love? I have been having a hard time with the sex witches…they pass like wax candles. My reflection freezes them…I want to make them still. But I trust how deep I have hurt. Pain, like this pool is pure with my hurt. My entire "spell" of pain (which could be pierian stream or song) I recognize that pain like the water is my accomplishment: love, depth, innocence, reality, reflection, pain.

IV

The first sentence can be seen in two ways—"e-raise" in the techno figure and literally "erase", which alludes to the rush of progress the friction of which makes the street disappear. I move in "ache of ma"" or calmness. I compare commas to people, then I abstract and say people erase and gather time; commas erase and gather pools. This abstraction stretches the concept in a very radical way. This is the metaphor abstract…a poetic tool to draw out the mind. Then I tell the reader they are time or "art I'm" Then further I sling time (as the stretch before) into elastic water (another poetic trick). Yet time that is reflective means knowledge…or memory. Then even more abstract "you can drink time,"…suggesting one can drink memory. And further…I am drained by a coma… or pause, or ache of ma. Where am I going? One stretch after another, huge stretches…totally unlike Jack? I say people must pause to love life…or our aching is a matter of love. Then commas space people out…literally meaning that the (,) spaces the sight out. What else? A super direct statement…the pool of time is crying upward. All of these statements are short and somewhat disjointed, direct and metaphoric…contrary of idea. But the result of the pool of time crying upward is rain or reign if things need to be in reverse to establish the kingdom. That time lived is in reverse like the rain is a poetic tool to change reality back from fantasy into "perspective". Why is it that there is no clock at the center of time? Why do no people have a heart? I emphasize that the "word" when put where there is no heart people see time. (This is a Jack sentence). So then I make time shiver outward to the edge of a comma. That is I am aware that

V

the word is the cause and time the effect of a word and this goes out into the comma or calm. If in essence it goes out into the comma then the word is made better. I am collecting the sound, after all what does a cause and effect like this sound like. There is no life and death. People whisper at the age, time made from the word, whispers with the pool. "Place" this truth. People should know what time is. Then the ironic sentence: "I am afraid to finish this poem…" That is, if I finish the poem I might end time.

VI

The tone of Jack is evident here. The idea that the "Sex Pistols" opens the Juke Box was a slurry way of saying sex opens boxes…yet more phonically it signifies the Jews coming out of the concentration camps armed with their sex/sects. A direct reflection "against" the previous pistols. Then a bunch of opinions from Jack, Chutzpa and moxie. When I wrote this it was responding to the previous poem…hence "channeling the click" refers to the picture being taken and the last word "click" of heels, button, and social group. The poem is mounding up like a wave…the aforementioned references and then into card play where the cards are connected by their colors to night, or four is force. Then "call me any time" is a funny remark…"I am any time" etc. which is a sustained theme in the book…time being disjointed and contrary. Jack states he is as well as his writing (which is a true statement). So this poem is full of quips and fragments all of which pump up the reader with attitude…diving deep into the soul, the bravado of who will laugh first and then sudden hate compared to the converse. And to finish the astronomy or O'rien, the sword, and a denial of replacement…that Diana cannot be replaced (the importance of the hunter). Then back to the Nazis: the Jews come out of the "box" with Sex Pistols, and Hermes gives Apollo the arrow tip to kill the Nazi's cryptically.

VII

This poem is for Brendan Murdock, artist, criminal, and friend currently in San Quentin State Prison for the crime of robbery. He is serving four years. We are interlocutors, our missives exchanged as strange and beautiful as the times. A while ago, before his incarceration, we went out for drinks. The first bar we went to he said, "when I go out I either fuck or I fight. By the second bar we hadn't found any female persuasion. So when Brendan is negotiating the bar scene a guy three times Brendan's size steps in during his focus upon a lone woman. Brendan steps back and whips his hand behind his jacket while stiff-arming the man in the face. Then he said, "I'm packin", and they faced off for some very long seconds until I came up and broke up the fight. We continued our reverie until I bumped into the big guy and he was motioning to his cocked bottle of Budweiser. I took Brendan out of the bar and we walked home…"I am packin" he said. Yet the poem is about the ref and God who awe are seeing on terms of fucking and fighting…both of whom if they are against us we shall teach this lesson.

VIII

Again time unknown begins this poem. Do we have to listen
to understand time? All musicianship (the sister of poetry)
is about listening. But not the way you think. I say unconceive your methods. Be alien. Be lost. Be forgetful. Then a
lesson/trick as a coin is introduced. How do we see? Is a coin
surface what we think? Keep flipping the coin…keep flipping
perception…until you choose your teacher. The books, Jack
states, allow "here" in every turn. Watch the book flip and the
pages choose a word. We are gamblers in a way. What word:
Now. If you are present and you flip your perception then you
are exactly stitched together with feeling. The poetic process
of seeing/feeling with a turn of phrase. When I say 1944, 1851,
and 2011…these three important dates of war separated by the
height of the Romantic Age, pre Industrial Revolution. Then the
language gets jibe and cool. When I say give me the bank, Jack
will give you the emptiness, the major value of philosophy/
poetry. Then you see one friend in reflection (Jack) and a billion
ways to un or not interpret life. Why? Because at this bank love
is life and life is won…perception is bank and it holds love and
life.

X

Then Jack shows up again…the irony of the problem being that there is no problem. I.e. we need problems to live. Admitting that we have fallen…they have fallen, clears the playing field. Again the pit, the very seed of the fall is a metaphor…to bear across to the vital or cross over. I explain the metaphor in a fruit and tree and tree "sound". This is the place of poets to think in. Then death as life and life as death and the "metaphor" the "bridge"…is the light of my soul uncorrupted. Yet the admission of the necessity of sinking into the pit/truth and knowing that there are no "sides", even no metaphor, yet there is just seed. I finish with seed because this is the core of life.

Ward Prologue

The ward poems were made with the intent to use my poetry as protection against black magic and other affront forces. I have found them to be particularly effective, but also beautiful in their ardent "repose" against the problem of life. Also they are very refined and raw, which lends each a potency that is, as a force, a rupture of the poem as weapon and defense. I level them at Nazis, ghosts, and other "projections". The truth in them is sharp and cuts both ways. Ward simply means, "to see".

Ward #1

I am a friend of nothing because if you realize the essence of
"nothing" you become more free. Since I am something we
cancel each other out: "nothing becomes something; something
nothing." The world's shit undoes my all. I admit myself as a
painting that the shit put on the wall and I'd "press" through.
Then I would un-become the museum…see the value of
nothing in this place of art. I am speechless. The cool feeling,
like pressing into the ocean, in the theater of art is art. I would
fall through the mirror like Alice. Here I would become the
Mad Hatter. My clock would tell every time…the existential
condition of some insanity. My words were subject to the
dissonance of saying. In the museum I grew. I realize L. Carroll
is saving Alice by his story. My grandfather and I float up
the Thames the same way, stitching with story the reality we
suffer/love. I admit that you can use words to save people. You
can "un" make your insanity. This is completely true as tested.
Then a complex sentence that uses negatives to play. Nothing
again assumes prominence over all. The poem is a painting of
water (I am, like Alice, looking over the side of the boat). We
are not docked (the painting of life is fake). Yet the water…here
where we look is real..

Ward #2

Having been on edge for some amount of years my poem
is now "looking every which way". I look multitudinal and
absolute. The reason why I am looking every which way is
because I am a trigger/switch of perception. People think I am
a dream…I admit that I am a real dream. When the shit goes
down my poem is exact as a trigger. My perfect eye waits. I
wait, poised. My poems are slow…my eye is fast. I would only
confess this if the other entity disturbing me were near. I have
a pure soul. I know that phenomena and myth exist. I know
that major "good" institutions are bad. My poem is the answer
to all of this…meaning I can not only answer but also save
myself with verse. I see the devil and the priest for what they
are. I focus and my muse is the bullet in the gun. My poetry is
protecting itself. I make a symbolic circle and I fire my bullet.
I blow smoke off the question…or gun. If you are a poet and
know the absolute you live. The demons are hideous. My ears
are purified by silver. This erases my guilt. I open my meaning
and "salt" (purifying) the story in a blanket of ocean or I clear
the O.

Ward #3

I am now playing with fantasy and reality. If I am a dream the "real" gun cannot hurt me. But the mechanisms in my hand are confusing. There are birds and a cross and a nine-millimeter Browning. I assign the birds to children, the priest the cross and my muse the gun. I talk of the symbolism of each. Poetry is a sign of gun here. All of these gifts erupt into play. I am naïve. The birds disturb my muse and she fires witlessly at the cross, a target for the church. The religious entities fall dead at the alter. I have accidentally killed the people who worship death. The envoy states: "Never accept a gift that you cannot live up to…" This is a pun that says in a round about way…if you are a priest and can live up to your symbol of death then you will die. And if I have a gun or a poem don't accept it unless you are capable of reading it.

Ward #4

Every poet, in the process of writing will be marked for life in some spiritual or figurative/material manner. I say I am anti-infinity because the established paranormal norm is to go for infinity, a representation of the ultimate timelessness. Yet we must have time lest we struggle forever without "measurement/health". I realize that I am being "made" by my life/poetry…so I must live for this; that is, I accept, after twenty-two years before the page and pen, my way. I also accept the words as my moment…or that time is made by numerous words in cycles of flow and perception. I try to measure my life with the number of words in the dictionary, but it is not enough. I discard this "time". I then focus all the words into a conversation of my spirit. The result is light! In voice, light that is sonic. It splinters the meaning (my existential and spiritual problem). I download my meaning into my spirit. At this point I am riveted and in the whirl of the poem and I evoke the angels, devils, sprites, Fairy, and elves. This is an ultimate poem of gravitas. I show myself to them as well light…so, in essence, I have drawn them to my brilliant well. Health of the phenomenal! The action causes an outward blitz effect. Then I say I am building myself alone (defiance…even in the face of these beings). In this "storm" I am one thing that I don't say directly, yet may be guessed as the desire of a child. I say the truth is unkind because in many realities it is. And the falseness (the made up) is special. Then I admit my love to my muse. At this spiritual/magical stage I open "true as the scintillating floral electric in my soul." It has taken all of this to admit my love…I have achieved the mystical and life ideal. This love is the word/ward.

Ward #5

I have found that often truth(s) are un-absolute. White absolute is the "un" or the negative/nothing of life. I "un" then everything. I accept "nothing". Nature and the church are better as nothing. And the truth is, is that ungodly acts are more "defined" than Godly ones. Is God disabled? I pray to those who are disabled. I say that God is behind the eyes of plague victims. I inform the church that invalids possess the word (which is true after their struggle). When we all see each other in jail (the admittance of these unstable times) the priest will come to anoint us. Yet when he is let in to the jail he will have to answer for his sins too. For there are priests who are indeed in jail. A Parkinson's victim will respond to the prayer. He will ask of the sins/achievements of the church—Africa, The Middle East, Spain, South America, Germany, and The Native Americans…all places of conversion. Yet how will the priest make the Parkinson's patient still?

This is a ward against the ignorance of the church..

Ward #6

Truth is slow. It takes out nails. It doesn't yes cars. It flunks emotional school (so difficult that it is). It has the sound of a radio. The waves take away its sureness of line. We must go slowly to gods. When I became a limpet I refer to Rich Doyle likening me to a limpet that holds fast to a rock. I hold on for life…the truth "holds on" (an oxymoron of energy) for life. The conned life is fused yet fast. It is like a flicker of a candle in a church. The light is con-fused by Jesus (blanketed or blank-it-ed). When you recognize the light/truth Jesus is unstrung. Snake like flickers that make him angelic (ironically, since the serpent is the opposite of holiness) I say he must burn with his pain. He represents how our future might be. I don't want o write this. "Don't show me a God I must think "through" to know." The light is the same as the snake's tongue ironically keeping him well…the idea of the Christian Religion…like prayers…that which is supposedly holy.

Ward #7

The most magical and pointedly bitter of my wards. I begin by
honesty (the stronger of the arts of introduction). I pull the ward
to the root of the tree or truth to "back see the slime"…or, to
defend the root by reversal. I say "fire" means "fire"…I mean or
the balance of the fire. Then I reflect the sickness to ward. Then
I reverse the sentence to create a double reflection (to counter
the sickness). After this I return to the word/ward. This I turn
slowly around the root. I clear conception by seeing nothing.
Conception sees nothing in you. If woven in poison this would
mean that the poison is made into nothing. I state, "Eat Me" and
its phonic double…what has been scary…the eating of Christ. I
want to know how you will do this…I also say when I ask you
get will. I submit 1851 (my defense) around the word. Defense
in that there are perfect books at the height of the Romantic
Era that ward the problem. Then I introduce Alice from Lewis
Carroll's story who I reflect against to counter hallucination.
Then I reverse again the black words of death so that the
throat is clear as Old English. And finally I say blind open and
clear as my line…so look! The main essence of a ward! And at
ultimate I face the problem and annihilate reflectively the "sick"
knowledge.

Ward #8

I address the snake (or evil). Then I set the snake up with my ferret and put him down the hole. Ferret's name is Deep Song. This is Lorca's muse. The hole does not go down…but rather up…perhaps to God. My poems, Snake, Game, and Deep Song are playing. The hole is an ass that goes up. The "ferret" is singing. The sounds are sexual…grunting etc. The snake is a poem. Then a space in time, like a pimp fucking his trick there is a ton of grunting. "Game" the thing the "snake" uses is fucking him over in the dark. I plunge my hope into the "ass" of the poem and Deep Song eats the ass of the snake, like a story. Then a poem comes out of the hole.

This ward is against anything that tries to take God. I plunge the problem with my poems. Now there is no problem with the poems and I am clear to see how this is poetic.

Ward #9

This is a set up ward. The poem is a weed, worth nothing, simple. It bears a "Happy New Year" sign. I am studying it, slow and deep like my love. It is a he. I am skeptical. It has appeared in the holiness of the lot (a pun). This poem is exciting to me because it is to solve, finally, my trouble with the attack on my poetry. I introduce God, a priest and an altar. I am anticipating holy light…a pun. Then "like a metaphor in the eyes of the Lord there is a varmint tugging, perhaps a gofer, at the root. The gofer is God, I think. Then, when the weed is pulled into the ground a device of poetry explodes. In this way I have protected the poetry.

Bulletproof
Love Song for the Makers I

Ironically I say this is a love song. I comment upon the makers
as lepers, my disgust with poorly made jobs. I suggest that
one should graph their bodies like the Man, my distaste for
authority. Yet I notice the peasants who are kings. I say write
like the plague/disaster to get to the kingdom. I am writing like
disaster. I detest the makers who are charlatan. I am a peasant.
My hands drip with future, the suggestion that the future is
poor…yet poor as the most rich thing. The makers, the fake
makers do not know what a "king" means. Cash fucked. Stuffed
with olive eyes of treachery. They promise the most profound
thing that only has death in it. I steal the knife from the table of
their making (the Last Supper) where Jesus is supposed to end.
I point to truth…"see how my fake direction is absolute"…the
North Star. I admit that as a peasant I am king…and I, Jesus,
put the knife up to the throat of God, the God that had let me be
crucified.

Love Song for the Makers II

My words are troping. Love is not a lure. As I have said, love is actually close to hate. I say that love is the pith or pit of hate when your back is against the wall. Impurity is the crowning achievement of purity. I am with my love and we are up against the wall. She turns a poetic move and I fall to the earth like milk (purity/birth) and I admit I am a fool to think I can save her (my love). Hence I am nothing. (She has saved me). I am lost. I hate losing. My fall is a fall of the fury of milk, my tears, upon the table. Fairy tears. I am up against the meaningless wall of love. Who will save me? I have lost everything. I am foolish as the words I cannot pronounce. My love drinks my white tears/ loss. I am alone in her womb...the milk of my fury safe within her.

Apollo Trade

This is a loyalty poem. The sun steps in and saves me. The sun
is Apollo's trade. This poem tells the poet how to be a hero, how
to not sacrifice but to take the blows for another that you love. I
am a poet and therefore my god is Apollo. When I fall I imagine
the setting sun. Am I reflecting Apollo? Is this how to learn to
be safe? I was without breath; I think that what I am falling
into—the ocean—is my rebirth. How do we know each other
enough to properly step in at the vital moment? The water is
worth more than anything…it is gold. The same gold in my
eyes. I conceive and everything drops. I become the water. I am
the setting sun. And here Apollo steps in at the last moment and
dives deep into my art. This poem is a recipe to save the poets,
my brothers.

Pixel Chick

I am sitting next to a woman who is "attached" to her comp.
She looks alien. I am interested in how she might be cloned,
what and if this is her religion. She is "fuzzy". I think of love
but cannot love her. How is she fit to the program of life? How
is she a "fix"? I think of how many dicks or detectives have "fit
her with worm". Has she saved anybody? Could she? I cannot
look at her properly…so I make her into a star, an imploded star
and watch her "egg" red in space pulse with power. I do not
understand this.

Virtues of Fantasy

Fantasy is real and reality false. This difference is thematic and
vital to a person who has slip-soled. I could not accept this for a
long time; after all there is only intellectual detection. Yet to accept
this statement is to realize that if fantasy is "real" then one can
shape reality beyond the material requisite. To notice this one will
find holes/slips in the language. Once noticed in the language,
this force that informs a person opens up the "whole question" of
actuality/truth/and art. If, for example, I say fantasy is real and
reality false I must also acknowledge that fantasy is false too…
which begets two similarities that cancel each other out—hence
real fantasy or the power to see language into "being". To live
in-between, where none is fantastic or real is hell and limbo. To
accept fantasy the "enchantment" of life may be artfully played
with, the building blocks disturbed and, ultimately the law
broken; for reason, the lifeblood of the law, cannot accept that it is
not real. To know this, however, begets the knowledge…one must
go beyond. To lose or forget "everything" is to be more capable
of these differences…because you have fallen. As fantasy requires
signs you are more capable of life like this by symbol relay…the
bridge again a metaphor. Once "through" and into the imagined I
see dark patches of glow, wet succulent water patting in refulgent
floor where "speech" resides. Here you become whole…moths
a-pulse (or mouths) with promise. You squeeze into the mark
and time becomes edible. (This is a realm of poetry). The seconds
on the clock are green…green time! Minutes become blue and
elongate in plumes in water. Obviously a boat appears and marks
of spirit shiver in the sails. We are going to deep into our new
wells and floral rivers. I am at home here. This is one part of the
kingdom I want to live in.

Confession of Terms

Words are lived. Indeed, if W. Burroughs is correct, they are viruses from outer space that "live on us". Like parasites we share life with them. They are not separate but unified with our actions. They depend upon us…like children and in order that we live they must live. My declarations here are false. I have had much doubt about language…even these aforementioned realizations. Poetically, however, I was trying to achieve courage to love and live with words no matter the rude design or assign above. Forgetfulness is seemingly the enemy of meaning, memory that is grasped by words. Here I am afraid that I will fail in forgetfulness. Hence, to say words/terms are what allows my love life, no matter parasite or virus, I am essentially saying that if words were made of excrement I would still want their possession. To have absolute trust at one's core is tantamount to trying to "hold" the language, something that must be done so that the "flow" is balanced, memory sated, and love won. I am saying that my absolute trust of language, no matter the problem, is what informs and makes my will capable of poetry/ speech/love. When one loses all, in this loss may be the greatest gain…the realization that emptiness is the cure for language's many states and statements. Not "having" language allows other, more sanguine perceptions to appear verbally. Hence, my desire here for life/language is satisfied by this wisdom. In this time one becomes tempered, becomes capable of both emptiness and deluge. My wit formed into sharp repose. I gained a deep understanding of time. My time fluxed (hence F. Kingdom) and I realized the purity of the edge gained by loss. When I realized this I pulled time or "now" and gave it to Apollo. This burned "purely" in the center of my heart. Then, from my "new" terms I drew my law. "I would live on my terms and my terms would live on my own terms (I had suffered for them) and my own terms would live on me on their own would live. Meaning…the trial of language, once overcome, allows the terms to live…on their own.

Loose

The muse (ic) is off. Poetry comes out my machine. I am
discursive and drunk as the ink spreads over in rainbows. On
nothing. Clear. I mention the sex witches (they live) they live by
their ass intake of pubescent suckers. Yet trouble brews in the
ink. The drink brews itself. I let them have it. I make a deep tea
of exact measures. I warn not to kill. No one out there knows.
I am happy to make them balance their desserts. They, I admit,
invade my body of song…they disturb. There is no love, no
rhythm. Not knowing how to love I tell them to imagine their
death in the beautiful halls (where they come from). These seem
like spells. Am I in a trance? I reverse Alice to un-trick the tricks.
Don't look at them…don't look at them seriously.

For the Prince

This is a poem for Prince William. I begin with milk, the moon, and mothers. Yet the words of the moon are black; this surrounds. The difference between the ink and night and milk and sun is that the milk or birth juice, when opened, is for life or sun. All women know this. When you look at the moon you are won. The night sky of ink surrounds this milk. I.e. the literature of the ages surrounds the symbol of the mother. This ink is absolute. You will ache loud or (a cloud) if your eyes go awry. Read through the veil or ink and you will find an ashen bride (death?) Still, the embers and stars crinkle in the veil. Then she is not there. "You must use the stars to see your queen." Do not look directly at her or you will see a wolf. If you know the right recipe to the stars you will defy death. (Or your wife). Kiss her and leave if you want to have a baby. Space, I say to William, has been waiting forever for the tremble of "tremendous" gratitude in your eyes…, which are wind.

Bulletproof

Having to look for a woman does not give me confidence. Yet this could be my muse…it can be un-centering looking for her. I admit that sex is both freedom and a chain. I am "sham-shackled" to the concept that love is a "possession". My luck, I say, is male; my encouragement is the page. I ask for the woman to be in the center. She will be the concept. She will be the possession. I will be the raw ink. I can see her…she moves worlds with her desire. I as impure as history. Read me, I say, deep as the world you are "looking" for. She is hateful. She is deadly as her want. Russian Roulette barrel turns. "What world will love you until you are bulletproof." My last poetic line.

Confession Purification

This was a difficult and necessary poem to write. I recognize
that nothing is secret. I gave away everything to free myself
from an oppression. I was attacked…a seven year deluge of
force against my will by a demon horde. I read the entire time.
This was the hardest thing I ever did. The words were a-storm.
I used the words every which way to counter the sickness.
Voices came in like a blitzkrieg (see opening poem). I tried to
measure my fury. I would not capitulate. I managed to reach
the center many times where everything stilled. I began to feel
purpose: light, warmth. Up until this time I fought with all my
might against a demon horde. This went down to my quick. I
wanted…all I wanted was my innocence. Love. I burned my
words in repose. Finally, when I had as much fight as I would
take I rested. I could do no more. I was very bitter, tired, and the
entire act was deadly.

Definition of Black

To finish with the table (a balance) with sun was my immediate impression. As king I input a love word. Connection versus correspondence is Jack Spicer's invention. The hinge would swing differently…. we would be loose. Connection is too close, too tight, to attached. I want to be loose. Yet I say connect me to the sun and there will be tides of deep memory. I am unsure. My pen drops rivulets of rhythm in this here (the sun)…magnetism. Read these sunspots as magnetic. Pull from magnetism purity. "Black is the meaning of life." I read this many times and cure (with my magnetism) into the purity of nothing. I prophesy that the universe is about to flip. Black is purity. They will be white and read…i.e. the story tells who are white and read. The black hole is not in the center. The black hole is on the edge. The center is not black but brilliance. If you turn the center (brilliance) right you will be the truth. In the center of death is a sun…now, love. I am your driver to this system. Fall upward if you are the mean of this myth to cleanse yourself. I say we are men. We are to the stars men (PKD). I mean are light is blackness.

I admit here, to finish, that the reverse is most often the right path. So my light is dark, my love is my hate, my fear is my courage, my hope is my doubt/faith, and my spirit is the scintillating brilliance of nothing.

Reich Deposition

A psychical force was bearing down upon me from 2004-2010.
I recognized the force as the "channel crossing" at Normandy
on June 6, 1944. D-Day. The realization that this was the most
pressing event of both the war and my family's survival
(England) moved me to assess that my psychical energy of
that war, to be specific, that fight, was the problem. If I could
depose the threat at the root of the problem I might realize my
health fully. This included the health of my entire family. So
I focused upon the psychical evil of the commanders of the
war. I could, I knew, rewrite the battle. From the indication
of the channel crossing poem to begin with I had, by writing
it, made the landing purely; purely of emotion, myth, purely
Fairy voice, purely of my hate. So from that "channel" through
the Jack Matter that was my truth given to me by Jack's
acknowledgement of my devotion to poetry, to the words
(defensive psychical against the beach "head"), to bulletproof…
my admittance of my foe and my reverse nature (black)…the
next move was to depose the major Nazis in the theater.

I lined up Hitler, Rommel, Goering, Eichmann, Himmler and
Goebbels. I put them at the beachhead in the landing spots in
the "bunkers" (to sleep well). Then I set free my pen/Lattarce
Aroshel and took them down one by one. That the attack is
cryptic and whimsical is their mistake, for I am serious and
exact. Within the poems, as artfully as I could dress a general,
I explain that the psychical force may be vanquished, but the
death queens who rear the engineered youth are still present in
today's theater. The poems are artful as the horded treasure of
the whole Nazi Party. That I attack the psychical force is telling

of how the mind may be invaded/possessed and "taken over" or cleared. My focus was to "clear" the mind, my own and my family and friends…by sheer psychical blitz.

Although they will need explanation they are here to stand on their own. There need be no rumination about them save for the simple reading of a battle.